The Boys from
Glee

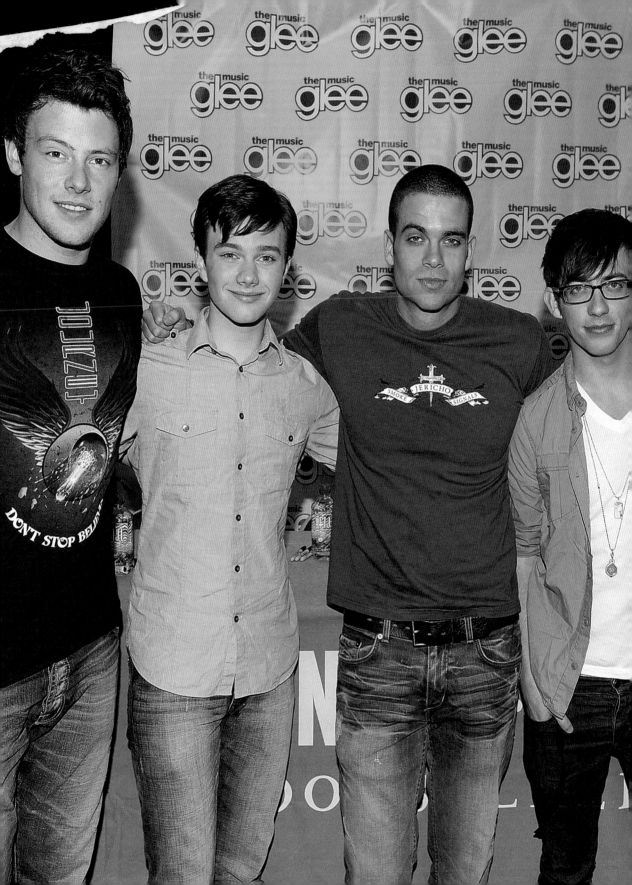

UNAUTHORISED

The **Boys** from

Glee

Inside
Out

MEL WILLIAMS

Piccadilly Press • London

Get Glee-ful!

Glee is one of the best TV shows out there – maybe *ever*! If you've been living on another planet and haven't seen it, it's a comedy-drama about a high-school Spanish teacher, Will Schuester, who is determined to transform the 'glee club' – school choir – and win national competitions. The show has everything: fab characters, great storylines, brilliant music, amazing dancing – and the cast are hot, hot, hot! Creators Ryan Murphy, Brad Falchuk and Ian Brennan searched high and low for the most talented, and gorgeous, young musical theatre stars in the whole USA . . . and it's safe to say they succeeded. If cute characters like jock Finn Hudson and nerd Artie Abrams make your heart skip a beat, just read on to find out what the actors who play them are like in real life . . .

Fast fact

The show is set at the fictional William McKinley High School in Lima, Ohio.

5

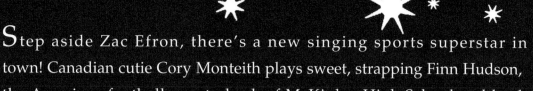

Step aside Zac Efron, there's a new singing sports superstar in town! Canadian cutie Cory Monteith plays sweet, strapping Finn Hudson, the American football quarterback of McKinley High School and lead male singer in the glee club.

QUICK QUIZ

Q) While living in Vancouver, who did Cory share an apartment with?

A) Fellow Canadian and 90210 star, Dustin Milligan

Full name: Cory Allan Monteith

Nickname: Monty

Birth: 11 May 1982 in Calgary, Alberta, Canada

Family: One brother – Shaun (older by 3 years), Mum – Ann McGregor and Dad – Joe (a serviceman), divorced when Cory was 7

Height: A mighty 1.91 metres (6ft 3 in)

Childhood: Cory and his brother were brought up by their mum in Victoria, British Columbia, Canada.

School: Cory didn't enjoy school! He dropped out in the ninth grade and tried jobs including being a greeter at a Walmart store, a cab driver, a school bus driver, and a roofer.

Start in acting: Although Cory played drums in a local band, he hadn't ever thought of acting until a casting director, Maureen Webb, saw him one day and told him he should try it. Cory has said: 'Three weeks later I moved to Vancouver with just a bag of T-shirts and two pairs of pants.' There, he did some modelling, dinner theatre, and landed small roles in TV programmes such as *Smallville* and *Supernatural,* and films like *Whisper* and *Deck the Halls*, before landing the role of Finn Hudson.

Fast fact

Cory's dad, Joe, has said: 'He was never a shy boy. He always liked to be out in the view of people.'

7

Finn Hudson

QUICK QUIZ

Q) What song did Cory sing at his in-person audition for Glee?

A) 'Honesty' by Billy Joel

CORY'S

GLEE CLUB CREDENTIALS

Cory landed an audition for *Glee* after sending the producers a video of himself playing on Tupperware containers using pencils for drumsticks! He then made the 20-hour drive from Vancouver to LA to try out in person. He slept by the side of the road in Oregon and learned Billy Joel's greatest hits and the songs in the musical *Rent* on the way, so he would have something to audition with! It's now impossible to imagine Finn being played by anyone else. But is Cory anything like Finn in real life?

Finn Hudson is a successful student at high school.
Cory is a school drop-out!

Finn Hudson plays the dream position of quarterback on the high school American football team.
Cory loves sports, but he prefers ice hockey and basketball to American football.

Finn Hudson is a singing superstar.
Cory's in-person audition for *Glee* was the first time he had ever sung in front of an audience. Cory loved music from an early age – his dad was into classical and he was always surrounded by music at home. Cory used to muck about on his dad's keyboards and was always making a noise on whatever was to hand, like running sticks up and down a fence. But Cory had no experience or training in musical theatre before *Glee*.

Cory's father, Joe, has said: 'He's a down-to-earth, honest type of person. It's not going to his head – fame has not gotten to him.' Cory himself has told journalists: 'I don't really party . . .' He has said he just likes to 'hang out with my homeboys.' Here's what else you need to know about this handsome, wholesome, Canadian boy-next-door.

Home

As a rising star, Cory is now based in tinseltown: Los Angeles.

Hobbies

In rare downtime Cory enjoys skimboarding, snowboarding, video games, and drumming.

Cory's faves

Fave colour: Blue

Fave food: Italian

Fave video game: *Call of Duty 4*

What last made him cry

A performance of the play *Equus.*

GET TO KNOW CORY

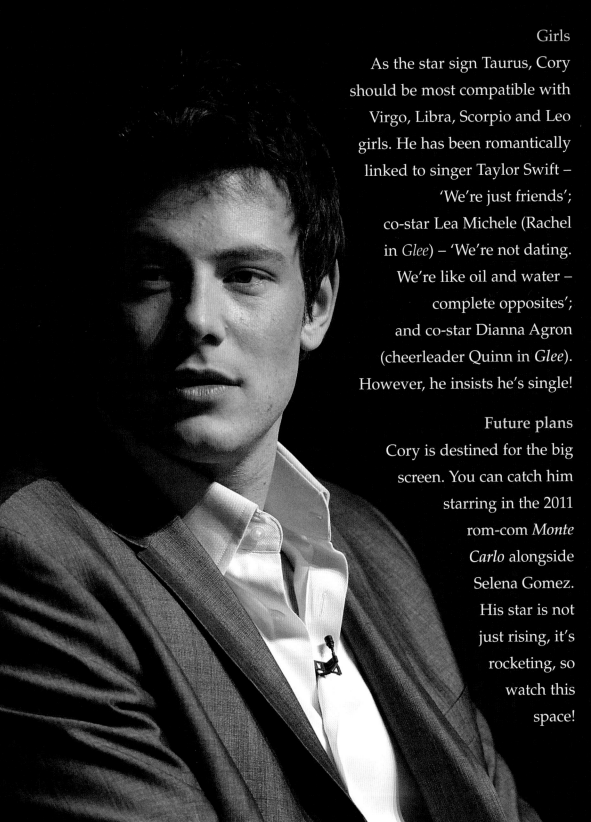

Girls

As the star sign Taurus, Cory should be most compatible with Virgo, Libra, Scorpio and Leo girls. He has been romantically linked to singer Taylor Swift – 'We're just friends'; co-star Lea Michele (Rachel in *Glee*) – 'We're not dating. We're like oil and water – complete opposites'; and co-star Dianna Agron (cheerleader Quinn in *Glee*). However, he insists he's single!

Future plans

Cory is destined for the big screen. You can catch him starring in the 2011 rom-com *Monte Carlo* alongside Selena Gomez. His star is not just rising, it's rocketing, so watch this space!

11

CORY SAYS . . .

On school: 'It wasn't for me. I can remember, ever since about the sixth or seventh grade, I just didn't understand why I had to learn what I was learning. For some reason, there was a spirit of rebellion in me.'

On life before *Glee*: Living in Vancouver, Cory said that he called himself 'a working-class actor. You know, you go from one one-line gig to the next one-line gig, to a couple of episodes on this show, a couple of episodes on that show, to a small part in a movie . . . I was making a good living. But it really wasn't a life.'

Trying to describe the show before it aired, Cory once said of *Glee*: 'It's as if *High School Musical* had been punched in the stomach and had its lunch money stolen.'

On bagging the role of Finn Hudson in *Glee*: 'I still feel like they've made a mistake and some day they're going to realise I'm the wrong guy for the job . . .'

Cory's favourite place to practise singing is in the shower. He has said: 'Sometimes I shower when I don't even need to – I get out when my voice starts to hurt!'

On going out with girls: 'I don't know where the time to date is these days!'

Cory with Taylor Swift

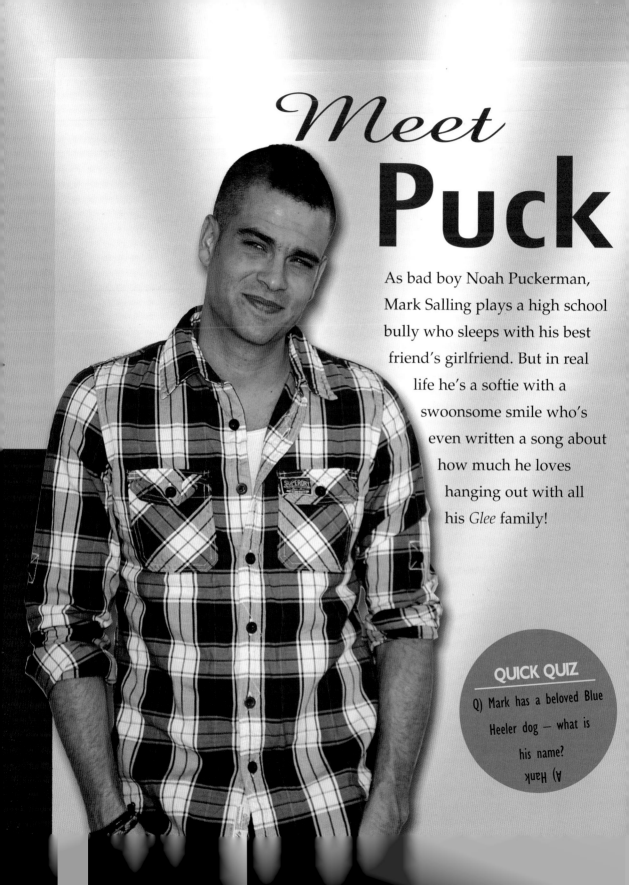

Meet
Puck

As bad boy Noah Puckerman, Mark Salling plays a high school bully who sleeps with his best friend's girlfriend. But in real life he's a softie with a swoonsome smile who's even written a song about how much he loves hanging out with all his *Glee* family!

QUICK QUIZ

Q) Mark has a beloved Blue Heeler dog — what is his name?

A) Hank

Full name:	Mark Wayne Salling
Birth:	17 August 1982 in Dallas, Texas, USA
Family:	Mum – Condy, Dad – John Salling Jnr, brother – Matthew
Height:	1.8 metres (5ft 11in)
Childhood:	Mark grew up in Dallas, Texas. His childhood passion wasn't acting but playing music. Mark began playing the piano when he was just 5, and started writing his own songs at the age of 7. He spent all his spare time playing guitar in local bands.
School:	Mark first attended Culver Military Academy, then graduated from Lake Highlands High School in 2001.
Start in acting:	Mark has said that he 'moved to Tinseltown with nothing but a suitcase and a guitar', hoping to make it in the music business. While trying to get a break, he attended the Los Angeles Music Academy and taught guitar lessons to pay the rent. As he was struggling for money, a couple of his students suggested he look for acting work too. Mark won small roles in 1996 horror film *Children of the Corn IV*, an episode of a TV Western called *Walker, Texas Ranger*, and another horror film, *The Graveyard*. Finally, Mark contacted around a hundred agents and, luckily, one of them called him up and put him forward for *Glee*.

MARK'S GLEE CLUB CREDENTIALS

Mark puts landing the part of Puck down to shaving his hair into a Mohawk for his audition. He thought the look might help him stand out from all the other hopefuls. He says, 'Lo and behold, it worked out. And now I'm stuck with it!' But is the haircut the only thing Mark and Puck have in common?

Puck is a great guitar player and singer. Mark is not just a talented guitar player and singer, he is a brilliant pianist and a gifted songwriter who has composed for other musicians, such as Josh Green and Danielle McKee.

Puck has a terrible reputation for being a womaniser and treating girls badly. Mark is an old-fashioned romantic. Once, to win the heart of a girl at his high school, he arranged little pebbles in a heart shape under a tree as a surprise for her.

Puck is Jewish, though not very religious. Mark's family are Christian and his religious faith influences his songwriting.

Get to know MARK

Puck is often mean and disruptive, but people who are lucky enough to know Mark well say he's quite the opposite. He's warm, caring and loves to be with friends, having fun.

Hobbies

If he's not filming *Glee* Mark is nearly always to be found behind a guitar or at a keyboard. When his mates can prise him away from his music, he likes playing frisbee, basketball, golf, and lifting weights in the gym.

Fast fact

Mark is an animal, bird and nature lover who volunteers at a local wildlife rescue sanctuary.

Mark Salling with actress Dianna Agron

Mark's faves

Fave music: Jazz

Fave food: Tex Mex

Fave movie: *Amadeus*

Fave TV shows: *The Simpsons*, *Family Guy*, and *Glee* of course!

What's on Mark's iPod?

Anything from Chopin to Elliott Smith, Pantera to Dave Matthews and Outkast.

Girls

Rumours have linked Mark with many beautiful girls, such as his *Glee* co-star Naya Rivera (Santana) and *The Hills'* Audrina Partridge. However, he describes himself as 'technically single'. Mark has said: 'My ideal girl should be sweet and considerate. Naturally beautiful. And anyone I'm going to commit to needs to have morals.'

Future plans

Mark has said: 'Hopefully I'll still be writing and recording music and I'll be on the show for as long as they'll have me – if I'm 35 and still in high school, so be it. I just want to keep growing as an artist.'

MARK SAYS . . .

On Puck: 'Puck has dreams of stardom, just like any other character in the club. He wants to get out of the town, and he has musical aspirations just like everyone else.'

On *Glee* mania: 'One lady brought us a baby to sign [during the Hot Topic tour]. She'd made a little *Glee* dress and we signed it, so that was unusual.'

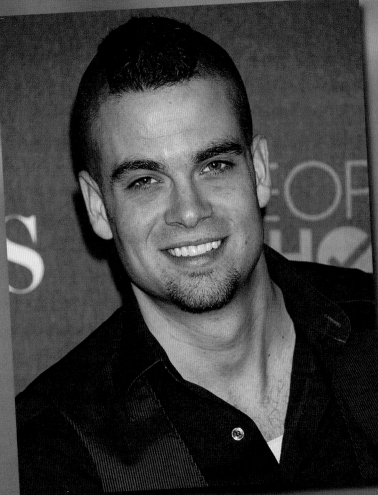

On becoming a musician: 'It was never a revelation I had, it was just what I did. Playing music was always a part of my life, I don't know anything else.'

On his haircut: 'I'm so over the Mohawk, I'm not gonna lie. It was cool for a while but, you know . . . I'm kind of over it. I feel better when I don't have it.'

On his *Glee* co-stars: 'Kevin, Naya, Jenna, and Chris – I probably hang out with them the most . . . and Lea. We're all pretty close though. We all know how to deal with each other and how to travel with each other. We're really like a family.'

On filming: 'We sit down between takes and I'll pull out my guitar and we'll all start singing songs – we really do . . .'

Fast fact

Mark plays in a band named Jericho. Their debut album is called 'Smoke Signals'.

Meet
Artie

Artie Abrams was paralysed from the waist down in a car accident when he was 8 years old. This adorable shy guy is played by Kevin McHale, whose natural geek chic is irresistible!

Full name:	Kevin Michael McHale
Nickname:	Special K
Birth:	14 June 1988 in Plano, Texas, USA
Family:	Kevin is close to his mum and dad. Older siblings include a sister – a showbusiness agent, who helped him get some early breaks in the business.
Height:	1.7 metres (5ft 7in)
Childhood:	Kevin has loved dancing and music for as long as he can remember. He says: 'My parents have a video of me, aged 6, at my sister's wedding, performing something from *The Lion King* in front of everyone at the reception. But I didn't think I could do that as a living. I wanted to be a meteorologist. I remember I used to put myself on tape doing the weather in front of the fireplace.'

School:	Graduated from Academy of the Canyons High School in Santa Clarita, California, in 2007.
Start in acting:	Kevin sang before he acted, although he always wanted to do both. From the age of 14 he was in a boy band called NLT (Not Like Them), who went on tour with the Pussycat Dolls, did a couple of songs with Timbaland, and had a guest appearance in *Bratz: The Movie*. Kevin also had small acting parts in *The Office* (as a pizza delivery boy), *True Blood*, and *Zoey 101*. In spring 2009, NLT ran out of steam (and money!) – just before Kevin got called to audition for *Glee*. He sang 'Let it Be' by the Beatles – and the rest is history . . .

Fast fact

Kevin's young nephew and niece, Jack and Rose Horan, are both child actors.

Artie Abrams

Fast fact

When the *Glee* actors and actresses were once asked who the best dancer was in the cast, they all said Kevin.

KEVIN'S

The casting team for *Glee* auditioned both able-bodied and disabled actors for the part of Artie before deciding that Kevin was perfect. He has said that his biggest challenge is remembering not to move his legs to the beat of any music: 'Everybody's singing and dancing and I'm trying not to move and it's the hardest thing . . .' But is Kevin like Artie in other ways?

Artie is a nerd who thinks he's cool.
Kevin says: 'I'm a complete nerd myself and I think I've always been drawn to those types in movies and on TV. So I was really able to tap into that part of myself quite easily.'

Artie is a social misfit at school because being in a wheelchair means he stands out as 'different'.
Kevin has said: 'I never had a real group – I was friends with everybody . . . high school wasn't bad for me.'

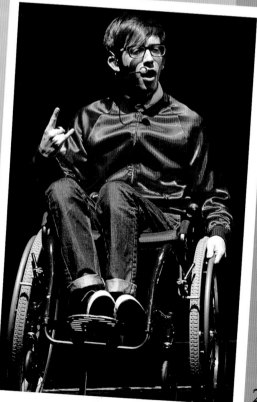

Artie is an amazing singer and is passionate about being in the Glee Club, no matter what anyone thinks.
Kevin has said: 'That's how I was. I didn't sing in school, but I always did it outside of school. And growing up, that's not always the coolest thing you can do. I never cared at all. I was like, this is what I like to do. You don't know what you like to do, I do, so . . .'

Get to know Kevin

Fast fact

Kevin listens to UK's Radio 1 while driving around LA. He loves DJs Scott Mills, Fearne Cotton and Chris Moyles.

So what's the supercutie behind the glasses really like? And yes, Artie's glasses are actually Kevin's own . . .

Kevin's faves

Fave colour: Royal blue

Fave musicians: McFly and Michael Jackson

Fave TV shows: *Skins* and *Brothers & Sisters*

Fave books: The *Harry Potter* series and Dan Brown thrillers, such as *The Da Vinci Code*

Fave food: 'Breakfast food'

Fave holiday place: 'Florida with my family and the guys'

What's on Kevin's iPod?

He likes everything from Radiohead to Bob Marley to Britney Spears. He says: 'I get sick of one type of music if I listen to it too long. So I switch a lot.'

Girls

Kevin has said: Artie 'is definitely more confident with the ladies than I am'! Are you anything like Tyra Banks? She's Kevin's celebrity crush.

Dreams

Kevin would love Sir Paul McCartney to appear on *Glee*. Also, he loved taking *Glee* on tour in the States, performing live before crowds of thousands of people. He has said he would love to do the same in Britain: 'My dream – to do Wembley or the O2. . .'

Kevin's secrets

He has two Beatles tattoos: 'Let It Be' on his wrist, and 'Imagine' on his ankle!

Meet **Kurt**

Fast fact

Aged 18, Chris played the lead in a short film called *Russel Fish: The Sausage and Eggs Incident*, about an awkward teenager who must pass a fitness test or lose his place at a top university.

Kurt Hummell stands out at McKinley High for being a self-styled fashionista with a soaring soprano voice and a crush on quarterback, Finn Hudson. Witty, confident and charming, despite being bullied on a daily basis, he is played by Chris Colfer.

Full name: Christopher Paul Colfer

Birth: 27 May 1990 in Fresno, California, USA

Family: Chris lives in Los Angeles with mum – Karyn, dad – Tim, and younger sister – Hannah.

Height: 1.71 metres (5 ft 7.5 in)

Childhood: Chris grew up in Clovis, California. His family have had a challenging time as his sister was diagnosed with severe epilepsy at the age of two and a half, and has been in and out of hospital all her life.

School: At Clovis East High School, Chris won speech and debating competitions, became president of the Writers' Club, editor of the school's literary magazine, and captain of a creative problem-solving organisation called Destination ImagiNation. He also wrote, directed and starred in a spoof version of the musical *Sweeney Todd* called *Shirley Todd*, in which the roles were gender reversed.

Start in acting: Chris has said that he knew he wanted to act 'from an embryo'. From the age of 8, he did community theatre – his first role was as Snoopy! As a teenager, he got a showbiz agent, and began going to LA regularly for auditions. After about 4 years, and trying out for about 30 roles, he won the part of Kurt . . .

CHRIS'S

Chris was desperately nervous about trying out for *Glee* because he grew up 'wanting to be' the show's creator, Ryan Murphy. Chris originally auditioned for Artie, singing 'Mr Cellophane', but although Kevin McHale was chosen for that particular role, Ryan was so impressed by Chris that he devised the character of Kurt especially for him.

Kurt is gay, and although this is accepted by his father, Burt, it causes his character many personal issues and conflicts, such as being bullied by the school football team.

Chris is also openly gay and has described his home town as 'conservative and anti-gay'. He has said that his parents were accepting of him but he was frequently bullied at school.

In one episode, Kurt is overjoyed at the thought of singing 'Defying Gravity' from the musical *Wicked*, but the solo is given to Rachel.

Fast fact

Ryan Murphy decided to call Chris's character Kurt because Chris once played the part of Kurt Von Trapp in an amateur production of *The Sound of Music*.

This is a real-life experience of Chris's which was written into the show. Although Chris wasn't allowed to sing the song in a high school talent show, his grandmother, a minister, let him sing the song in her church instead.

Chris says . . .

'There's probably more of Kurt in me than I'm willing to admit, but I really wish I could be more like Kurt. I wish I could walk into a room and have that Ryan Murphy air of superiority about me.'

Get to know CHRIS

Chris's first job

Chris used to work at a dry cleaner's in the summer holidays during high school.

Hobbies

Chris regularly practises wielding a pair of sai – swords used in martial arts.
He says, 'I'm kind of a ninja.'

Chris's faves

Fave TV show: *Nurse Jackie.*
Fave music: Black Eyed Peas, Lady Gaga, Broadway musicals, film soundtracks.

Chris's secrets

The scar on the left side of his neck is from surgery in 1998. Also, in 2007, he lost
over 40 pounds in weight thanks to 'horrible methods called diet and exercise'.

Dreams

Chris has said: 'I really want to be Pinocchio, if Disney ever did *Pinocchio* on Broadway. Actually, some of my fans I think started a Facebook petition for me to do that. But I would love to do it, maybe in between seasons of *Glee*. It's always been a goal.'

QUICK QUIZ

Q) Which celebrity would Chris most like to appear on *Glee*?

A) Chris longs for the musical legend Julie Andrews to come on the show and play Kurt's fashionable grandmother.

Meet
Will
Schuester

The sweet, caring director of the Glee Club, Will Schuester, is played by Justin Timberlake-lookalike Matt Morrison.

Full name:	Matthew James Morrison
Nickname:	Matty Fresh, Triple Threat (meaning he's good at singing, dancing AND acting)
Height:	1.83 metres (6 ft)
Birth/family:	Matt was born on 30 October 1978 at Fort Ord Army Base, California, USA, as both his parents were military nurses. The family moved a lot with the army and eventually settled in California.
Childhood:	Aged 10, Matt spent his summer holiday with a cousin in Arizona, going to a theatre group, and decided he wanted to be a performer. From then on he did youth theatre and dance school.
School:	Matt won places at the famous Orange County High School of the Arts, then New York City's Tisch School of the Arts. However, he dropped out of college when he got himself an agent and successfully auditioned for *Footloose* on Broadway.
Acting career:	Matt has had an illustrious career in both musical and 'serious' theatre (e.g. *Hairspray, The Rocky Horror Show, South Pacific, The Light in the Piazza*). He guest-starred in TV shows and films (e.g. *Sex and the City, Ghost Whisperer, CSI Miami*) before *Glee*.

QUICK QUIZ

Q) In 2001, Matt was a member of a boyband — what were they called?

A) LMNT (he described the experience as 'the worst year of my life'!)

MATTHEW'S

GLEE CLUB CREDENTIALS

QUICK QUIZ

Q) What is Matthew allergic to?

A) Cats

Matthew says . . .

'If I could have created a TV show for myself, this would have been it . . . It's great to see the crossover of Broadway on television.'

Will Schuester is a teacher at his former school. To cast the character, *Glee* creator Ryan Murphy spent three months studying actors on Broadway, where he found Matt. Matt has said that, when he auditioned, he 'didn't try to belt out a big show-stopper. I came in and sang "Over the Rainbow", accompanying myself on the ukulele. I guess it worked.'

Will is a Spanish teacher, but his passion is for musical theatre – he is determined to return his old Glee Club to its former glory.

Matt has said: 'It's kind of what my life would have been if I hadn't gone to New York and been successful there – I would probably have been a choir teacher, or something like that.'

Will is a surprisingly good rapper!

Matt has said that he grew up loving street music – he used to be great at break-dancing and hip-hop.

When Will was at high school, his Glee Club performances won national competitions.

Matt has won countless awards, including the 2009 Satellite Award for Best Actor in a Series, Comedy or Musical, and nominations for the Best Actor award at the 2009 Golden Globes and 2010 Emmys, all for *Glee*.

Matthew Morrison

Get to know Matthew

Glee becoming a worldwide phenomenon, Matt has said: 'I'm kind of ~red of fame, because you lose your life to it. I would be fine just playing ~d parts. I just want to make a living doing this, and I'm happy that I've ~ able to so far.' He relies on his friends to keep him grounded, and has ~ 'They're the strongest, most loyal group that anyone could ask for . . . ~'t know where I would be without them.' So what else is important to ~nulti-talented star?

Hobbies

Matt loves skydiving and boxing. But when he's in a show he conce[...]
less strenuous hobbies like reading and watching movies.

Matt's faves

Fave musical: Stephen Sondheim's *The Assassins*
Fave TV show: *24*

Girls

Matt's first celeb crush was Tiffani-Amber
Thiessen from *Saved by the Bell*. He was
engaged for a short while to actress Chrishell
Stause of US soap opera, *All My Children*.

Matthew's secrets

While at college, he worked at Gap.
He has also been a singing waiter
in an Italian restaurant –
he didn't mind too much
because he got great tips!

Future plans

Matt would like to play a villain
for a change, because his looks
always cast him as a good guy.
Other than that, he has said:
'I'm living my dream. If I
could do anything else though,
I would want to be a midwife,
like my father.' (His dad is one of
only about 50 male midwives
in the USA.)

Meet
Jesse St. James

Glee creator Ryan Murphy describes Jesse St. James as a miva – a male diva. The pompous, competitive, lead singer of Vocal Adrenaline is played by Jonathan Groff who's used to playing sweet and innocent!

Full name: Jonathan Drew Groff

Birth: 26 March 1985 in Lancaster, Pennsylvania, USA

Family: Father – Jim, a harness horse trainer and driver. Mother – Julie, a gym teacher. One older brother – David.

Childhood: Jonathan had a strict Christian upbringing. His parents were very sporty – they were stars of their basketball teams in high school – but Jonathan always preferred performing. At the age of three, he watched the Disney musical movie *Mary Poppins* six times a day. Jonathan took part in a lot of community and school theatre projects and worked part-time on the crew at the Fulton Opera House.

School: Jonathan graduated from Conestoga Valley High School in 2003. While thinking about applying to college, he impulsively caught a bus to New York City and began going for auditions. He landed the role of Rolf in a revival of *The Sound of Music* and never made it to university.

Acting career: Jonathan made a name for himself in theatre on and off Broadway, including performing in *Fame*, *In My Life* and *Spring Awakening*. On TV, he regularly played Henry Mackler on ABC soap opera *One Life to Live* before being cast to guest-star on *Glee*.

Jonathan's GLEE CLUB CREDENTIALS

Jesse is often seen in a vivid pink Vocal Adrenaline shirt, with black braces and trousers.

Jonathan grew up near Lancaster, where there are Amish communities. He thinks that Jesse's outfits are very similar in style to Amish menswear – shirts (sometimes in a vivid blue) with black braces and trousers.

Jesse's female rival – and one-time love interest – is Rachel Berry. Rachel is played by Lea Michele, who played the female lead opposite Jonathan in the stage musical *Spring Awakening* for nearly two years. Jonathan has said that Lea is his best friend and has commented that working with her on *Glee* has 'been a blast'.

Personal stats:

Jonathan's three favourite TV shows are *Alias, Lost* and *I Love Lucy*.

In downtime, he loves long-distance running.

Previous jobs have included being a waiter at The Chelsea Grill in Hell's Kitchen, the voice of the Wishing Well at an amusement park called Dutch Wonderland, and teaching acting to 11 and 12-year-olds at a theatre camp in Pennsylvania.

If Jonathan had not become an actor, he would have become a teacher.

Jonathan's secret is that he never swears.

Fast fact

Jonathan didn't have to audition for *Glee* because Ryan Murphy created the part of Jesse especially for him — they knew each other because they had previously worked together.

Meet Mike Chang

When Harry Shum Jnr auditioned for *Glee*, it was just for a day-player deal. That turned into a few days, then a week, and then 20-odd episodes . . . and now his character even has a name – Mike Chang!

Full name: Harry Shum Jnr

Family: Harry's father is from Fujian province, China, and his mother was born in Hong Kong.

Birth: 28 April 1982 in Limon, Costa Rica, where his parents had moved to open a business.

School: Harry started acting in middle school. He didn't dance until late into high school.

Stage career: Harry's first job was as the only male dancer on US TV series *Comic View*. Since then, he has been a lead dancer for stars such as Beyoncé, Mariah Carey, Jennifer Lopez and Jessica Simpson. He has been a dancing silhouette for iPod adverts and appeared in the movies *Stomp the Yard*, *You Got Served*, and *Step Up 2: The Streets*. He has also had countless jobs as a choreographer, such as for the Oscars.

Harry's

Mike Chang is a jock-turned-dancer. Harry was a high school sportsman too, when his track-and-field buddies once dared him to audition for the school dance company. He actually did it – and from then on, dancing was his passion.

Personal stats:

Harry speaks English, Chinese and Spanish.

Harry adopted a stray dog that he found on the set of *Glee* whom he named Charlie.

Harry supports the charity Invisible Children, which works against the abduction of children in Uganda.

Harry says . . .

'Dancing fulfils my soul!'

45

Only the beginning . . .

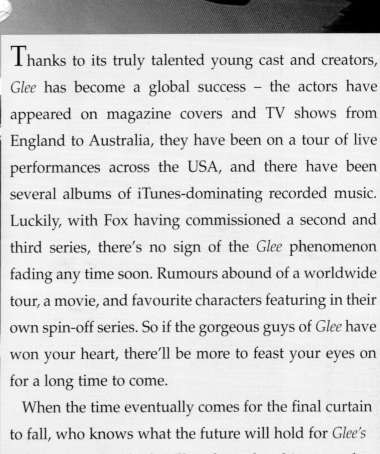

Thanks to its truly talented young cast and creators, *Glee* has become a global success – the actors have appeared on magazine covers and TV shows from England to Australia, they have been on a tour of live performances across the USA, and there have been several albums of iTunes-dominating recorded music. Luckily, with Fox having commissioned a second and third series, there's no sign of the *Glee* phenomenon fading any time soon. Rumours abound of a worldwide tour, a movie, and favourite characters featuring in their own spin-off series. So if the gorgeous guys of *Glee* have won your heart, there'll be more to feast your eyes on for a long time to come.

When the time eventually comes for the final curtain to fall, who knows what the future will hold for *Glee's* young stars? Surely they'll go from showbiz strength to strength . . . But as Will Schuester himself once said: 'Who cares what happens when we get there, when the getting there has been so much fun?'

Fast fact

In 2010, Glee was nominated for 19 Emmy Awards — more than any other regular TV series. At the Golden Globes, it won the award for Best TV Series — Musical or Comedy.

First published in Great Britain in 2010 by Piccadilly Press Ltd,
5 Castle Road, London NW1 8PR www.piccadillypress.co.uk

Designed by Simon Davis. Printed and bound in Italy by Printer Trento srl
ISBN: 978 1 84812 137 9

1 3 5 7 9 10 8 6 4 2